WHO ARE WE

Atmosphere Press

WHO ARE WE

Man and Cosmology

AN ESSAY IN VERSE

OBSERVATIONS AND INQUIRIES

WILLIAM GUEST

The Universe is Poetry – Man its Grandest Stanza

CONTENTS

This book is dedicated to the memory of

ROBIN McCORQUODALE

poet, novelist, artist, wonderful person and my partner for a brief 2.5 years until her death in July 2014. Robin gave support to me by the excellence of her talent and by her attentive and sustained interest.

PREFACE

Know then thyself, presume not God to scan;
The proper study of mankind is man.

- Alexander Pope, An Essay on Man: Epistle II

P.1

Poor Man. The aching weight of the heavy question.

Rich Man. Climbing the hills of comprehension.

What question could be so big, so necessary

To know its answer, to plague him, drive him?

Whether long ago, or in our age, we have pined

To know about this,

Our place in our Universe.

P.2

Here, the question and its answer will be proposed.

This must be said: Man arrived recently into the Universe

By Evolution. Are we ready to ask and answer?

This depends on what we've become, who we are,

What we've learned. Read the answer to see

If you think we're ready

To know the answer?

P.3

Of course, you say, doesn't every age believe

Its time has come to ask and answer?

The cave man? Clearly we did not know enough.

Five hundred years ago the Scientific Revolution began

Erupting, a catapult to give needed height.

P.4

Not every human being on Earth can see.
The infant, senile, mentally ill, ones who suffer
Poverty, ignorance, lack of education – they cannot,
Never could or will. Is this misfortune, or spared the prod?
Who among us can genuinely seek to know?
Always humanity has its layers of who participates.

P.5

This I believe. There comes a time
When Man on Earth can say
This is the question, and this is the answer.
Oh, certainly not in all details,
But sure enough to pass the tests.
When and how do we know that we know?

THE QUESTION

*The power to question is the basis of all
human progress.*

- Indira Gandhi

1.1
Do we know everything? No,
Of course not. But do we know enough
To answer who we are, where we came from?
Yes. We can say that much about a dog or horse.
So what we know now about Man is enough
Surely to yield the question and answer.

1.2
What question should top the list?
Do we know enough to rank the questions?
It clearly should be a question that we can answer,
At least in large part. We, we lucky ones, have arrived
At sufficient knowledge to feel we know, at last,
The major points to connect the dots.

1.3
Here it is: a question in three parts,
But one question overall.
Where did we come from?
Who (or what) are we?
Where are we going?

1.4

Gauguin wrote this at the bottom of a painting
Of a Tahitian scene, fraught with symbolism,
Saying: here is Man, and Life, raw and primitive,
And this puzzles the brain. We are burning
To know the answers. All of us want to know.
Seeing that question, on that painting, said to me:
Yes, that is the top question that thrashes in our heads.

1.5

Before Man, did anything matter? After Man?
Suppose the only thing that ever happened
Was the appearance of one bubble. And suppose
This one bubble then popped away. No bubble remains
To care that it was once a bubble. We are a bubble
Happening now. And we care now, a lot. Never mind
That this will be lost in Time.

1.6

Oh curiosity! Need to know, desire to know!
It generates us, drives us, blossoms us.
Knowledge is an endless garden of wondrous fruit.
As fruit-cravers we are loose inside the garden.
Can fruit explain fruit; or cravers explain craving?

1.7

I wonder what a question is. I'll ask.
How could it arise at all? A puzzle, perplexity.
Then choose. Do we want to seek to know? Are we
Even free to dumbly walk away? As Man we evolved
To have no choice, bound to seek to know. Could Man
Arrive on Earth, become aware, presto-like, and take
A look about, without stumbling on a question?

1.8

An answer needs its question. Without the question,
An answer wanders orphan-like.
How surprised we are that we are.
We can explain the mosquito and the dinosaur.
Now as Man on Earth, we seek ourselves.

1.9

A question needs to have an answer. Otherwise
It's like a leap with no place to land. But there's more.
The answer must come from a competent source. Tested,
Proven. No question can be chosen
If it cannot have an answer that can pass
The tests.

1.10

Is the Scientific Method, when it's proper, the test?
This genie from a cloudburst of the Scientific
And Industrial Revolution came almost like magic
Falling into our hands. We cannot say it answers
And tests every question, or that it's the sole path
To truth and discovery, but it has no apology to make.

1.11

The bountiful fruit of knowledge and technology
That emerge from the Scientific Method
Is our way of learning how things have evolved,
What they and we are made of, how it works, and will work.
They rank at or near the top
Of Man's seminal achievements.

1.12

You see, that's the premise of my case
And the answer that you will read. If you accept it,
Even if only in part, then we are together.
I know no other way to persuade that Man
Knows the question, and the answer is now emerging.
You are the jury to whom my case is submitted.

1.13

There are many candidates sprouting from mushy,
Evolving, happy-sad, dreamy-perplexed Man-alive.
How to live forever, disease-free? Many are not questions,
But quests. A question is a way of saying "explain this"
Or "what is that," not, I want to make a change:
How to be happy, how to be rich.

1.14

It may not be the biggest question that some universe
Could pose, or some star, or some photon, or some rose.
Here we're discussing Man, that sublimely supreme creature
That has skyrocketed to a level high beyond his myriad
Relatives in Life. Beyond even our power to dream. We know
There are dreams. Beyond what we can dream.

1.15

Most of us feel, coming through our windows and doors,
Drafts of wondering – pounding gales for some –
This fact of being alive, here and now, being what
We seem to be, doing what we do. It begs to be understood.
If only we could have it handed to us,
A chiseled tablet, or a Rosetta Stone, that could explain it,
Explain it all.

1.16

There are questions that cannot qualify.
What is the meaning of Life? It's often said that way,
But to ask what is meaning is meaningless. What
Is in the mind when we seek the meaning of Life?
To glean meaning there must be a frame of reference,
A system outside of us. We know of no external system.
We wish for one, but we know of none.

1.17

Wanting meaning in things we do, our work or goals,
Is different. There's a context of society, friends, family,
And the mores, history, culture of life, for comparing
Our actions and thoughts, to seek to piece together
Relevance, usefulness, in reference to all of that. But
Who we are as Man on Earth in the Universe,
Our Beginning, our Purpose, our Death, our Destiny?
That's wholly different. What's the context for that?

1.18

Ripeness is essential. Granting, if you will, the question
That is most important is the one identified herein, we know
That, say, twenty thousand years ago, it would have been
Impossible to grasp, and address with any hope
Of identifying it, and explicating a believable answer.
Modern Man, certainly in the past few centuries,
Has felt ready enough. We are now on the cusp,
Although it's still in order to rock in our chair,
And wonder.

1.19

What is here for us is Science, the Scientific Method,
A forest of fruit for five hundred years, dazzling
Us with understanding our place, the Universe,
Our Earth, its processes, Life, its provenance,
And most of all, of course, the origin and nature
Of us: Man on Earth, Earth in the Solar System,
Our Solar System within our Universe,
Our Universe and its dynamics. So much
We know now that was darkness yesterday.

1.20

We do not know the full and final answer.
But we can sniff it, taste it, see its parts, and feel
That it's okay now to rejoice, now we have it
Somewhere within our net, the joy of a capture
Happening now in the history of Life on Earth.
Since long ago we've wanted to answer Who Are We,
That's for sure, and maybe now the time is now.

PERSPECTIVE

Science is a way of life. Science is a perspective.
Science is the process that takes us from confusion
to understanding.

-Brian Greene

2.1

In all of Time and Space, when and where
Would you choose to anchor an intelligent thing?
I mean, suppose you were a god with power
To arrange such things? Where would you
Put this Man – we'll call him that –
And would you grant to him knowledge
Of his where and when and what?

2.2

Think of the options. One way to begin
Would be to create energy and matter,
Lots of it, and let it roil and roll, spreading
Across somewhere, for billions of years.
When everything's ready, put him on a planet,
A rocky sphere with water, orbiting a burning ball.
Make his origin some microbial life and let him earn his way
Out of the swamp. Make him yearn to reach pinnacles,
But do not give him a map –
Leave him alone.

2.3
Now, suppose that's your plan. Stick him
On that ordinary planet. Let him grow like yeast
From a microbial culture, snarling and snaking
Up the ladder of prowess, where hands, teeth,
Arms, legs and brains thrive or perish, kill and eat
Kindred life to stay alive, making sure to tag the process
With a blind, obsessive compulsion to make more and more
Of his own kind.

2.4
Let Life evolve through a few billion years of desperate
Struggle and chance, and when Man himself appears,
Evolving from the ever-so-slow survival-of-fittest,
Out of the rawness of Life's mishmash, let him ponder
What he is. Let him peer out upon his place
And wonder: Where am I? What's going on?

2.5
What you could do with this thinking man is this.
First, let him think that where his homestead sits
Is everything. Let him think that yesterday,
Today and tomorrow are all that matter,
Strung into little years. His history is the generations
He can remember. Let his world sit still for a while.

2.6

Let him play a while with stories of floods
And let him engage his time searching the Earth
For the garden of his beginning. Let him see
Across a field and stream, marvel at the size
Of mountains and oceans, be amazed
At the lights at night in the sky. Would you finally
Let him know from his tiny blip of place
How huge was Time before he arrived?
The hugeness of what surrounds his place?

2.7

Would you, after a while, give him peeks
Of reality? Give him wisdom to feel
The enormity of distances measured
In light years? Open his mind
To sense the length of a billion years?
Would you let him find out how
His Earth was made, how long it took?

2.8

Would he find out about the Big Bang?
Billions of galaxies, each made of billions
Of stars, all like a cauldron of matter
And energy, and possibly something
Much more mysterious and dark than that,
Waiting for him to figure it out?

2.9

Maybe it's better that way, the slow
Realization that he is such a tiny thing,
Made from a super flux of Life evolving
Upon a spot so miniscule it's hard to believe.
Like slowly getting used to cold water in a lake
And finding it's not so bad, in fact
The pleasure is stimulating and grand.

2.10

What is the lesson from this story?
To know where we came from,
Who we are, and where we're going,
Requires absolutely pushing our awareness
To reaches far beyond how we normally think.
If we don't, we don't get there.

2.11

If we would know our place in the Universe
We must ponder hard the breadth and depth
Of what we've begun to see through the parting veil,
Saying over and over – it's big. Really really big.
And grasp this frame of Time and Space to see
Where and when our beginning began.

2.12

And one thing more. The how of it. Life
Appeared as a microscopic wiggle, something
That's deeper than we know at this stage.
But we know a lot – that it happened.
And something about when on Earth –
Markers along a timeline of Evolution.

2.13

And how Evolution pushes so hard,
Gnashes mercilessly, prunes beautifully,
Shows off its successes, declaring a success
To be anything that survives. When it is, it is,
And is what it is. Can we, should we, will we
Tamper with that?

2.14

This plan could be a way to do it
The dough
The oven
The recipe
Life and Man
On Earth

THE BEGINNING,
THE MIDDLE, THE END

Man must rise above the Earth - to the top of the atmosphere, and beyond - for only thus will he fully understand the world in which he lives.

- Socrates

3.1

Come with me now, to a place above our Universe
Where we'll float like a cloud, our observation perch.
Time and Space will play before our eyes
So we can have cognition of everything anywhere anytime.
Look at that bang! Look, look. See those galaxies forming!
See that tiny spot, just there. It's a planet. It's called Earth!
Are you curious to know how we could happen to be,
From a single bang?

3.2

All matter and energy that we can track and analyze,
All of our Universe, spewed from then until now, still swelling
On and out. Track it back by imagination, un-swelling it,
To smaller and smaller, darker and darker, denser and denser.
From that little near-nothing began this bursting.

3.3

What's a beginning? In reality (pardon the word),
It cannot exist in any mind. Every beginning
That we know has its history. Beginnings and endings
Are ways we think, because of the need for slicing
One event or string from another. Time and space
Have no boundaries known to us. An absolute beginning
Is much beyond our ability to conceive, the same as ending,
Eternity,
Or nothing.

3.4

Notice the concept of before, or after,
Or such sequence words. Our minds use relationships,
Causes, effects, processes. But something's lacking.
What was before the Bing Bang? Without empiricism,
Facts as litmus, we have theory. Like moths,
Theory is our light.
The switch-on of much of what we've found,
The light-bulb turning on.

3.5

Within a century's cascade of physics and astronomy,
The Big Bang theory was born and validated, hard science
Fingering the puzzle pieces to montage the picture
Of our physical universe – atoms and particles seething
Within the early hot caldron, matter and energy transforming
Into star-stuffed galaxies zooming outward from the center
At panic speed, stars thicker than mushrooms
In the morning's forest floor
After a nurturing rain.

3.6
Theories supply the air that science breathes.
That moment when the Higgs boson was only theory
Gleaned through keyhole spying into the underworld
Of particle physics, and our need to know
How mass is made, or transferred across boundaries.
A theory even before we had the tools to test.
But the moment came, decades later,
Into the next century, for champagne toasting.
Need to know? *O reason not the need!*

3.7
A man's reach should exceed his grasp, and lo:
The idea of cosmic inflation, a sweeping, swelling
Of let's-call-it space, like a tsunami at mystic speed and range,
Transforming, transcending, faster than the speed of light,
Flotsam floating inside, and spawning Big Bangs –
One of them
Beginning our Universe.

3.8
That's an idea, one of several, having math
On its side, with glimmers of clues we see today,
Through our grand telescopes with grander dreams,
Informing us of our home, peering into the deep
For dark energy and dark matter, vibrating strings,
Matter and energy beyond dimensions we can see.
A tool. A tool. My kingdom for a tool!

3.9

We will leave aside until maybe some future
The question of what was before cosmic inflation.
Except this tale of a post-lecture dialogue
Between the little old lady and Richard Feynman
When she riposted to him that everybody knows
The world stands on the back of a turtle.
He asked her, but Madam what does the turtle stand on?
Not to miss a beat, she said, another turtle of course.
When he asked her again and again, she closed it by saying,
Dr. Feynman, it's turtles,
All the way to the bottom.

3.10

But we must persist, searching for the bottom turtle.
What's before before? What's the component of that?
It's solid within our bones
To want to know, and never stop wanting.
Even with no sure hope of proof we press our nose
Against the window pane.

3.11

Pause for a moment. Our existence – just this simple,
Naked, stark fact staring at us this moment from the mirror –
Inside this Universe, or maybe something larger, we exist.
This mere fact alone, is itself more than can be said
Or celebrated. Man arrives on Earth, takes a look around
With wondrous tools, minds, dedication –
A dazzle of existence.

3.12

We are not done with the mountains of conundrums
Blocking our peering for what we wish to see,
Some of which is fated to remain beyond our brains
And tools. Are there other universes? There's room enough.
They may have happened an eternity ago, or will happen
In the eternity to come. Or more may be pulsing now
Inside our present eternity.

3.13

Here in our subjective selves
We ponder only one. Good lord, isn't it daunting
Enough to figure this one out? But figuring this one out
Leads on, and on, and on, give or take a bang. Once
Upon a recent time we thought our Universe was small
And static. Hubble came along and saw. Want to talk about
Inconceivable scale and velocity?

3.14

Right now, as I write, people are gathered
In a small café in Paris, talking, drinking wine, eating.
I know them not, and never will, but they exist
In their place in Time, and I, over here, in my place.
On other earths, or in other universes, some form of life,
Maybe giant leaps ahead of our grandeur (we think so),
May be there, like we are here. Or they were there,
Or will be there, like we are here, for our few moments
Of fame.

3.15

Thinking of other universes means thinking on and on –
No possible limit to bump against. But you cannot avoid
That other question of what, when, and where, is nothing?
Surely there's some edge. Does it exist any place at all,
And what is place? If so, does it begin somewhere?
Does it end somewhere? How far, how big the stretch
Of human mind?

3.16

Unless you want to think that nothing does not exist,
There was always something. Always is longer
Than our brains can travel. We use the words infinity,
Eternity, forever, always – but that's as hard as grasping
Nothing, even as just a border. To say that there was always
Something is the same perplexity as saying
There once was nothing.

3.17

Space is not the nothing; space has features, like curvatures,
Undulations, energy phantoms, acting and re-acting, creating
And destroying, coming and going exactly like ghosts do it,
Even harboring the mysteries of what it was, or what it is,
That sparked the concoction that flowered into this Universe.
It may be that it's nothing that does not exist.

3.18

And this something we have, which we're part of,
Also has motion, this motion that can stiff-arm gravity
And bring a halt to its clumping ways just by swirling.
Imagine. Motion with no stopping. What if
There were no motion, ever? But there is.
As the lights came up in our big tent, there it is:
The greatest show began to perform! Our Universe!
See it swell, and tumble, and rumble, and roar.

3.19

How do you make a star? Is it from a starter kit?
Wandering atoms of hydrogen heed the horn of gravity,
Bleating together to flock into a swirling disk.
The center ignites. What fusion, what chemical
And plasma spasms, stars of many sizes (as though
The size of any star is graspable), many born and gone,
Many yet to come. Stars dance around their playground,
More wonders than even children could imagine
During an eternal recess.

3.20

Amazing, this motion. What makes motion?
Nature abhors disparity. Heat and pressure crave to equalize.
Because of this, the something has motion. But for this,
Would there be stasis forever? Hot moves to cold, pressure
From high to low. Add gravity and a few other mysteries
To this mix, and voila! The Universe becomes
A motion picture show.

3.21

So let's go on with this show, our very own Big Bang.
Man's entrance cue finally comes; his window has a view.
Such volume, distances, fireworks, fantastics – colliding,
Exploding – gargantuan power hiding in black holes,
Jets of exotics in streams more aptly envisioned as screams,
Supernovas that manufacture in a galactic instant
Elements that add to what star-factories feverishly churn out
Unceasingly.

3.22

Man enters the Universe in its Middle Age
When galaxies have formed and are visible to us,
Before they recede beyond view. Inside our Milky Way,
Inside our solar neighborhood, we bask under that sun
Up there, our sun, which is half-way gone. A mid-size star
At its mid-life stage. In our pea-patch galaxy.

3.23

Joining the performance in the happy mid-life
Of our Universe, Life on Earth found its niche
In this Goldilocks good fortune.
If you want to get mystical,
This is a moment.

3.24

Here and now, in the bloom of our dreams
And knowledge, we see what we can see,
Do what we can do, within the walls
Of science. Outside these walls we cannot explore
Our hunger, scratch the itches of our theories.
From the parapets where we stand
Our visions are birds
Flying under the moon.

3.25

Note the matter clumped into that ball orbiting that star.
See Earth's beginning, and follow it to Life's beginning.
Are we there yet? Not yet. Not yet. Be patient
Another billion years. The Earth must accumulate,
Boil and bake, shimmer and shake. Hot molten interior,
Crust outside, a pie in a ball. Agonies and ecstasies
Rampaging in geological melodramas. That little planet?
Such a lonely tiny place, a roll in the dice
Of non-existence.

3.26

Four basic forces comprise the energy wellspring.
Gravity is intractable. We have formulas to describe
Its behavior, but what it is, we don't know. An unknown
Equation curmudgeon, a pervading filler of space, curving
Universe lanes. There are many wondrous phenomena
Out there, known and speculated, and ones still hiding as well.
Aren't we lucky
To know what we know?
And to search for the rest?

3.27

In a micro cellar we find the Weak Force. Well, of course.
But also in such a place we find the Strong Force.
That we harnessed and used. First we used it to kill humans
Massively for the sake of avoiding more massive killing.
Universe, did you intend this basic micro force
To be co-opted? You needed it as your super-glue.
Are you surprised that Man arrived
And will not be denied?

3.28

Electromagnetism is the fourth force, recondite
Magnetics and electric charges, the chemistry
Of atoms and molecules, the building blocks
Of everything. My eye looks at my finger.
See, the finger is nothing but electromagnetic
Binding of atoms into little things that make
My finger. And my eye. Now we could ask
What is a finger and what is an eye?

3.29

Newton and Einstein gazed upon a world
That makes sense, but quantum mechanics
Knows about topsy-turvy. Schrodinger must
Be dealt with because, think what we might,
His explanations work. Show me the person
Who does not wonder how the reality of particle physics
Can be what it claims to be. Maybe it's reality itself
That is in two places at the same time,
Or wants to be.

3.30

And what is Time? Time is change. All the pulling apart,
Pressing together, collapsing, exploding, energy and matter,
Interacting, spreading – veritably orgiastic
For billions of years
With one aspiration – boil, mix and change. Interact and build
Exotic new elements, which in turn will interact and build
New exciting molecules, which in turn will - - -
On and on.

3.31

Well, we see a lot of past and present. Turn now to the future
Of our Universe. When we see the pitcher release a baseball
Toward home plate, we know the ball's future.
It will not change unless by instant intervention
Of some force not known to Man.
But it may slice, or dip, or curve inside or out, or meet a hit,
Or not, which make statistics for projecting that kind of future.
Such knowledge of the future is not complete,
But it sure is a lot.

3.32

So is it that simple to foresee the future of the Universe?
All we have to do (wink) is grasp the trajectory of everything
That moves, and factor in the ambient forces that will shape
The paths of things in motion. Like planning tomorrow's trip
With a map. But we're talking its far future, not ours.
We will not be in that picture. And no one will call balls
And strikes, And no home runs.
No crowd to roar. No one to hear the silence.

3.33

Play it again, Sam.
How to even glimpse a future with no end?
We speculate about entropy, heat swallowed by cold.
Stars burn out, becoming cold, dark and dead.
Imagine. Every star, all warm planets, and anything
Carrying heat, in every galaxy in all of our Universe,
Becoming cold, dark and dead. the leftover junkyard
Sprawling across regions reached by everlasting expansion.
Tell me again, where does heat go
When it disappears
From the Universe's grave?

WHERE DID WE COME FROM?

I will here give a brief sketch of the progress
of opinion on the Origin of Species.

\- Charles Darwin, *The Origin of Species*

4.1

That beginning of seminal glory emerged

When a few lifeless chemicals, bathed in liquids,

Bonded as a system and slowly pulled upon itself

The mantle of replication and the prowess

To manipulate change to meet opportunity.

If it were not so, it could not be so.

4.2

Sprinkle molecule bits like dust in the Universe,

Tiny specks of Life, or the grist for making Life.

You may ask, what is Life? It's absolutely impossible

That it exists, of course, but it happened anyway.

Some creature somewhere may yet understand

The alchemy petri dish wherein molecules unite

And learn to dance, may even hear the music

Or see some process doodle out the steps. When we see

The eye of a fly or the bloom of a flower, there it is:

A bowl of light and a self unfurling.

4.3

How can this meager brain stretch to feel what Earth and Life
Have known? Continents of churning shifting crust floating
About the globe, mountains rising and falling, volcanoes
Erupting like monsters from the netherworld,
Temperature and atmosphere never sure of what to do.
Life engaging in this heat and cold of battle, hunkering down
Like insurgents, with a single-vision strategy – survive –
And there was no second place. What kinds of limbs and beaks
Did not matter if they worked. Havoc of land and water
Over vast eons:
Watch as Life prevails.

4.4

Several times, some type of mass extinction
Gave heavy blows, big ones, nearly wiping out Life.
One such devastation covered the Earth
Seven hundred million years ago. Ice
Around the entire globe, in places the thickness of miles.
A big one, all Life gone, a false start, the end of Life on Earth.
Poof.
A snowball Earth.

4.5

Except: tiny microbes beneath the ice struggled on.
The Earth, this little rocky planet not far from the sun,
Recovered. Let the process resume; let Life roil and roll
And thrive. Yes it did. Think about it. Seven hundred million
Years ago. Can you think a thousand years? A million?
Seven hundred million years is a long long time.

4.6

Those microscopic bits that happen in many concoctions
Of start-ups, that chemistry (we know so much chemistry)
That seeps and tangles and simmers – we can look at it
Happening, and still not know how it happens.
We can make a bit of Life jump alive, but we must use
A starter-kit from some shelf – a secret way
Of formulating stuff.
Then the stuff, that oozy bitty baby stuff, it comes alive.
Yes, it becomes Life!

4.7

I say we do not know how to make a bit of Life.
You could say, that's laughable. You can say,
We experience Life with all of our senses and brain.
We can watch it form, see it born,
Function, live and die. We study Species,
The Kingdom of Species, know all their properties,
Past, present and future. We know what Life is.
How far down deep into a thing
Do we need to go to know that we know
What it is?

4.8

While skiffing water-ways in the Amazon Basin,
Along the seams of lush forests, I marveled to see green limbs,
Like the necks of baby birds, craning to their stretching limits
For more, and the forest itself fermenting, crackling.
There abounded a desperation as though Being
Is not enough. What drives this?
What pre-primeval force?

4.9

Evolution? How does it work? Many ways, of course.
It's so obvious, Thomas Huxley even saying
It was supremely stupid not to have seen it.
Contemporaries were seeing it, and it had been foreseen
In glimpsing insights. But it was Charles Darwin,
After long meticulous vineyard labor, whose hand
Wrote the book so clearly and persuasively –
The Origin of Species.

4.10

Darwin did not even know about genes and DNA,
The micro mechanisms that make and remake and modify.
He did know, and explained, that a living thing is suited,
Or not, to cope with its environment that constantly changes,
So the offspring variations find niches and luck, pursuing
Relentlessly the compulsion of reproduction, honing skills
Like sharpening nails and teeth, stealth, camouflage, flight,
And power, for killing, for food and water.
Survive, survive, survive.

4.11

But Darwin did not explain Life, how it opens.
No one has. The beginning of a life is the greatest of all –
The "it" that grabs onto existence at one blinding,
Vanishing flash, like catching hold of a moonbeam
Just in time. Wanting to.
But what wants to, and what compels?
Every bit of every living thing has its moment to begin to Be.
Such a load of wonder to say
With a breathless word or two.

4.12

That unknown has stumped us so far – us, the makers
Of machines, electronics, medicines – us, the species
So bursting in music, poetry, technology, explorations,
Space travel. . . Yet, we are stumped. We know not
What Life is –
The very thing we are!

4.13

Imagine a cave man saying on this point: hey, man,
What do you mean? Figure out what Life is,
While I'm dressed in animal skins, eating flesh
From the cave floor? How many of us today
Are dressed in animal skins, eating from the floor
Of our cave?
We still don't know.

4.14

What's going on? Down there, where the happening
Is forged? If we say it's stardust, we must go beyond
The stardust and ask, what is that? How did it happen?
What is happening right now? Bits of something, smaller
Than microscopes can see, as though they know –
A conspiracy, a plot, the most single-minded purpose ever.
Do it. Do Life. Be Life. Reach, expand, grow, against all odds,
More awesome than awesome.
Something is going on.

ALONG CAME MAN

From far, from eve and morning
And on twelve-winded sky,
The stuff of life to knit me
Blew hither: here am I.

- A. E. Housman, A Shropshire Lad, xxxii

5.1

Well, what is Man?

From off the table in a lab, that is, on Earth,

Man suddenly found that he existed!

What? I see I hear I feel I smell I taste

I talk I think! What is this? To be this I am?

5.2

We became aware, and aware of being aware.

We did not know what we became until we became.

As we emerged, we took stock of what we are,

We did this slowly, based on Man's Calendar.

It happened in a quick wake-up moment

Based on Universe Time.

5.3

If we look at an acre of land and walk around it,

That's Man's Calendar, in terms of space, compared

To what we know of the reaches of the Universe. Scanning

The Universe, compared to scanning our acre of Earth,

Reveals a scale where processes and events unfold

At a pace our one-acre minds can only pretend to fathom.

5.4

Move the pointer on the grid of Universe Time –
Way over to the right side – toward the zone of now
Where you and I are, right now. Far smaller
Than looking at the whole fourteen billion years.
We're just a sliver of a sliver – you need a magnifying glass.
And you'll sense that Man's playpen in Time
Is so scant even in its fullness.

5.5

Look back, way back, to Life's first tangles and fusions:
That stuff that spewed out from the biggest bang,
And when the time and place came round
An automated procreating devastating wiggle
Higgled waves after waves in sea on land –
A short time, really, a small place, surely.

5.6

Man is orbits higher than all myriad forms of life,
Feasting and ruling, night and day.
What if, let's say, no kind of man had ever come to be?
Plants and animals would sprawl in tooth and claw
Slowly grinding out a saga eons long, and the stories
Of the Universe would not be told. Imagine if the stories
Of the Universe could not be told. Not by anything, ever.

5.7

Evolution master-minded everything, having its way,
Brooking no dissent. A cell from something, a something
Into something, the next seed to plant, the next plant to seed;
Evolution has its labor. A direction? Roulette wheels inside
Roulette wheels inside roulette wheels. What if, somewhere
Back there, at the pass, at the crook, at the freeze,
At the thaw, at the flood, when asteroids came,
At one cataclysm or another,
Something quite different had fluked?

5.8

It's very strange, if you want to think about it this way,
That only one species made it to the level of abstract thinking,
Reasoning, technology, the way of Man. A countless number
Of species, having land, water and air, and yet, none of them
Ever got beyond living at the mercy of taking ruthless nature
On the chin. It must be a hard road to travel –
The one we took.

5.9

Evolution does not think. It did not choose to make
What it made, or to make only one. It is none other
Than a process, dynamic, a lottery. So, is the making of one,
Just one, vanishingly unlikely? There was a beginning
That became a cascade, which happened to hit upon us.
It seems that Man had many triggering spurts,
The luck of repeated lottery wins. What does it take to win?
Evolution, wipe that knowing smile off your face,
Or is it just your smirk?

5.10

If Evolution's twirl had hiccupped now and then
Would it have been trees, or not, us, or not?
Life as we know it, times twenty, or us still squirming
From cell to cell? Fortunately for us the only thing
That happened is the only thing that happened.
Our evolution's tale is told, as surely as past is past.

5.11

Life doesn't care. It has a reckless disregard when its quest
Is growth, survival, thriving, stretching, replicating.
It spreads, yearns, dreams, ever reaching to make a twig,
To find a perch, to use every resource
Of light, water, nutrient –
Like water rushes downhill, heat plunges to cold.
Look at a sprig of grass.
You know what's on its mind.

5.12

Who are "we"? Surely not the micro cell? Or the ape
We came from? We need to have a starting point?
My parents? Or do we go back
As far as my great grandparents
To say, that's me? No, my lineage is darkened somewhere
Back there in the human flow. But I will not say it is the ape
Or micro cell. Somewhere closer to me. When humans
Got dressed in modern attributes – there we began.
Enough of the right kinds, so that we can calmly say
We are like them.

5.13

What attributes to put in that package? Walk upright,
Fire, tools, language, bury the dead, abstract thought,
Art – a long exciting list. Some came to us sooner than others.
The winner's accumulations completed the package
Inside the Cro-Magnons in Southern Europe 25,000 years ago
(Add or take five thousand years or so, does not matter).
Before that, no species had it all complete.

5.14

If I could have, I would have held the dim, flickering light
For that grandfather while he was painting bulls
On the cave walls of Lascaux, or any of those hundreds
Of mystery art-painted caves (Yes, mystical too).
We would talk of what we're doing, and why.
In the stretching labyrinths
Of our brains, still seeking more light. I would ask him,
What is our future? Learning about survival,
About joy, to laugh, and also cry.

5.15

Also my hunter grandfather, many generations removed.
Later another one taught me to farm, another one, to read
And write. Beget, beget! I am, I think, I learn and teach.
I dream, invent, create, build, plunder and kill, destroy,
And build again. We govern ourselves like little boats
In perpetual storms. Dream, and dream again.
Life, those seeds
That begat my grandfathers, accumulated also the will to live,
To struggle, to thrive, while in denial of death. Dreaming
We live, and always will.

5.16

So, that's the story. Happened in a sliver of a thin slice
Of all that Time. We awake in our state of exalted
Consciousness. Aware. At long last. Exalted awareness.
What are we? What is awareness? Mosquitos? Snakes?
Whales? Monkeys? Homo sapiens, one hundred thousand
Years ago? Aware? Of what? Is it, now we've become aware
That we are aware,
That we are amazing, at last?

5.17

Of course, even this modern-model primate had ancestors
Through millions of years, who left for us to see
Tracks and detritus, jigsaw puzzles with many missing pieces.
Our deep desire to seek, to learn. Who can doubt we crave
To know where we came from? Look at our learning today,
Compared to five hundred years ago.
Five thousand years ago?

5.18

During the last minute or so – I mean, the last
Thirty thousand years – how have we changed?
Evolution gifted us with good anatomy. We could outlast
The game we chased. We have vocal chords, we learned
That symbols could communicate, which is to say,
It's not the thing itself, it's a thing that points the brain
To another thing, or thought, or feeling. Ah,
I have it. Abstract thinking! So simple, so critical,
So huge. We leapt ahead of all other animals and primates.
That reflection I see is not another man.
It's me myself.

5.19

We won the race to become the Modern Man.
Neanderthals perished, our closest kin, who struggled
So valiantly and vainly to stay alive. I have a sinking spell
When I grasp that from time to time whole civilizations
Became extinct, vanishing. So how to feel to know
That a whole species that was close to us was abducted
Into oblivion? Who will mourn the passing when
Our turn comes to vanish?

5.20

Like hopscotch but with a path, our modern ancestors
Meandered from caves and hunting into farming and villages,
Social networks. Once upon a time a lowly tradesman
In the Euphrates Valley, doing nothing but packing caravans
Of goods to send from here to there, did not realize
That his wet clay marks, when dried and sent along to keep
His drivers accountable,
Invented writing.

5.21

Oh, serendipity with such power and glory! Writing!
Unintended. Five thousand years ago, a blazing light.
Now, even with hindsight, we cannot assess its worth.
The information age dawning in the last micro-second
Of time that we're in? Writing gave legs to a beast
Ready to run.

5.22

Writing. The archives of civilizations, like none ever before.
Writing. Connecting communities, spreading information.
Writing. Ideas, art, learning, commerce, government.
Without it,
We had only speech, signals, symbols conveyed in painting,
Sculpture. To think of words, to send a word, to save a word,
And the fruit of writing words. What a giant leap
For Mankind!

5.23

A mere five hundred years ago the Scientific Revolution
Began to swarm across the land.
That beginning had its history too. The cradle of civilization,
A bonanza. The Greek Civilization, in that island of Time –
An unbelievable brilliance, almost good enough to tempt
History to end the novel. Oh,
The Romans – grand achievers who knew
They were invincible, until they weren't.

5.24

Here and there the hopscotch continued. Byzantium
Art and mathematics. Over in China and Egypt,
Their flames rose high. In Europe, the cruel
Middle Ages, laying in the hunger that would launch
A rocket – the Renaissance, which had been seething
Underneath, and the sky lit up.

5.25

Now the trumpet horns for Science and its Methods.
It would take too long, too many are left out.
Who remembers Bruno, burned at the stake
In sixteen hundred for heretically saying
The Earth was not the center of our Universe?
Ah, Copernicus, the wily one, the wit to publish his fantasy
Upon his deathbed. Galileo, a brilliant and obsessed
Man, destined to be a star.

5.26

The list is long. Shakespeare, Newton, Beethoven,
Darwin, Marie Curie, Einstein. And the age of discovery –
Columbus, Magellan – getting acquainted with the geography
Of planet Earth, the distance around it. We could sit all day,
And more, just writing names. And what a long list,
To this day, in a feeding frenzy, feasting at the festival
Of science, exploration, and discovery.

5.27

If it were Wall Street speak, we would call it a bubble.
How can it go any bigger? Just the last few hundred years
Shining like a blast of light, a supernova of humanity.
And we can swell with pride. It is us, who lordly survey
Out kingdom planet and the Universe, our minds wrapping
Around Life Itself, where we are king almighty.

5.28

It's come to this high moment. We know, at least
Enough to say we know. What's that you ask?
Are we the Greeks? The Romans? Alexander the Great,
Who wept when he believed he had conquered all there was
To be conquered? Do we look for the truth of truth,
At this center of where we are? Could it be we are the new
Deluded ones?

WHAT ARE WE?

The force that through the green fuse drives the flower
Drives my green age; that blasts the roots of trees
Is my destroyer. And I am dumb to tell the crooked rose
My youth is bent by the same wintry fever.

- Dylan Thomas

6.1

Fourteen billion years ago: the Universe. Five billion:
Planet Earth. Four billion: Life. Thirty thousand years ago:
Modern Man. The greatest of these is Man. We, and only we,
Have the podium. From all of Life only Man ascended
To such phenomenal grandeur. What are we?
We are Universe, Earth, Life, Modern Man.

6.2

I celebrate with exuberance that I have a mind,
That Evolution of Life on Earth has brought my mind
To understand much of what we are and surely the joys
Of what we are. Compared to what? Compared to
What might have been? My mind, a mosquito?
A baboon? A trout? No, no, no. Whatever I might have been,
I am glad for what I am.

6.3

It's strange, how our lineage got loose, a surpassing animal –
Although much like our kindred – except we alone
Kept getting ahead, bit by bit. At first, we used
That same old playbook of survival, holding it close by –
Using long long Time to work and work, connecting
Advantage to advantage.
Some advantages were rockets.
And we became Modern Man,
With more rockets ever since.

6.4

So, imagine, if you can (and you and I are of them/of us)
What if this renegade power-seeker, this winner of frequent
Evolution jackpots, had never had jackpot tickets,
Or had squandered his jackpot winnings, then
We would still be there, in the wild, jumping from ground
To tree, to munch or flee, maybe messing with tigers
And elephants on their terms. Or, like countless ones,
We might not be here at all.

6.5

No need to doubt it. This could have not happened.
Not a single edge we gained was ever guaranteed.
Oh, but it did happen! We rose and rose and rose.
Where were the giant leaps, the biggest ones, and the many
Slow small creeping ways to go up? Which is better?
Countless smalls, or now and then, giant leaps? Of course,
Everything that ever happens has its history, its offering
To the future.

6.6
How do we write the joy of Life on Earth? The victory
Of survival. By imagination can we view a blank Earth
Battered and beaten by asteroids, volcanoes, extreme
Weather? I cannot imagine the absence of me, a me that
Never happened. Even more, I cannot imagine the "what if"
Of no more Life, after its start-up, that pure miracle, and then
– Pop –
Magnificent Life, all gone.

6.7
Our slow-motion, grainy selves paint Life's whole canvas
With illusion and reality, hope and denial, myth and longing,
The overwhelming bone-soaked joy-and-pain
Of awareness and being. We are a walk-on in a drama,
Seemingly no beginning, no plot, and no end. To love it
Is like a trance that cannot be broken, the way we have it,
Or it has us.

6.8
Evolution willy-nilly gold-gifted at our door
The curiosity and intellect that call us to understand.
Whatever phenomena may fill another planet,
I'll take this one that tugs and stretches us to
The many mountain-peaks, the climbing of them,
To achieve the perches. More and more to come, to seek,
Maybe to find something, and then . . . die we must,
Each of us, every one.

6.9

I say all of this, and could go on for years, because I am
A human being. I am Life, and Life am I. Evolution,
Here I go again. I can't help but love me and my kind?
But Evolution, you made me to do this. It's true, clearly true,
Isn't it, that every kind loves its kind?
The bear, wolf, bee, bird,
Fish, microbe, elephant, whale, penguin,
The soaring eagle?

6.10

I asked a dog: tell me dog, what's your dream
Of the best form of life to be? What would you choose?
For surely you see us humans strut and fly so high.
In his way he answers back: a dog is the best of all.
At night I dream of dogs and love my dog ways.
I am a dog. I cannot choose another way.

6.11

If only the dog, the horse, the fish, could be empowered
Like us to celebrate itself! What wonders, what excitement,
What visions, what self-love would it display? I am a cat,
And watch me pounce! I am a fish, with color and grace
And delicious moves! Or even the tree, reaching to the high
Of light, rejoicing in green and limbs and leaves.
What is this called?

6.12

The human experience is deep, wide, long, high –
Think boundless. Write write write sing sing sing
Dance dance dance paint paint paint, Say it, babble it,
Capture it, explain it, wonder at it, praise it, enjoy it,
Know it, feel it. It changes across its surface. Ripples
And bubbles from its currents, and when we are saying
It again, saying it all again, the long-fingered probes
Into ourselves, we move on to more, being Human,
Struggling, crawling, flying, hoping.

6.13

The way it works is: Human sperm meets Human egg.
It's that simple. Not even hello. The door is open. Indifferent
To who are you or what's your family, or is this love or rape?
No, some other place may pay attention, but these are not
Concerns for what sperm and egg are made to do. But
What happens next is most surprising.
Every time.

6.14

The prowl of sperm, the nest of egg, a life is opened,
Beginning, gathering nourishment the Universe
Has spread like petals along its path, seizing
Its moment to thrive, to become, to experience being alive,
To reach for the glory of being a life, to feel and know
In a brief tick of Time
The high of being I am.

6.15

What brought you here you newborn human child?
A moment ago you did not exist, but look at you now.
What do you know, and how do all your pieces work?
A gene for this, a tongue for that, a cry for appetite.
What's inside your skin-bag, stocked so full?
Don't answer now – I'll wait until you know.

6.16

You may well say, I never asked to be born. What a way
To come to be! Some kind of cornucopia of bodies, limbs,
Hisses and kisses by two people seeking thrills,
Then little micro bits tangled and fused.
Not quite sure of when the I of me emerged.
Nobody asked me if it would be my choice to be.

6.17

I am a camera. I'm twisting and stretching and crawling,
Trying to take a picture of myself, or even to take a picture
Of myself taking a picture of myself. To no avail.
Oh, I see. I'll take a picture of other cameras taking pictures
Of other cameras, and with a leap of reasoning: we're all alike.
I know who I am by knowing who they are.
Who are they?

6.18

While talking to you I have had a million cells die
And be replaced. My heart has beaten a thousand times,
Moving blood and all kinds of cells around among into
My body parts, food processing, water filtering.
In my quiet brain, neurons have had fireworks,
Probably enjoying the show. Am I the same person talking
With you a few minutes ago, a few simple words? Look!
I have a hook, to use to reach in and capture me, a still life,
Just so. Oh, what am I?

6.19

Compare my brain to the millions of other species,
Or just primates. Measure and tap the functions.
What glows in the dark, when I blink or think?
A mere malfunction of a piece of tissue can cause
Bizarre aberrations in what I do or don't do.
No normal brain exists – only countless variations
On the idea of normal. And it changes from birth
To death. To be Human is to be an approximation.

6.20

Did I say consciousness? If so, a mistake. It's too much
To understand. Studies and literature grow like mushrooms,
And yet, the last book so far still says: What is it? How
Does microscopic matter-and-energy-based biology
Crank out the stuff we call consciousness? I ask
Consciousness: What are you? And it answers back:
I am the you who is now searching to know who you are.
Look at you searching for you.

6.21

How many ways we have for coping with reality!
Explanations for why we're here at all. No problem.
Belief systems, invented, taught, passed on, myths
That cradle us so we don't cry, to help us go on.
What structures, or make-believes, or cocoons,
Do we concoct in our rattletrap meanderings?
Some of us may know reality. Those who think you do,
Please, raise your hands!

6.22

Oh paradox! How it comes to us, if "this" then not "that."
But it is "that"! Oh stupid brain! Or is it, what comes to us
Across the threshold, mixed in ways the brain cannot handle,
Gets stumped, really stumped? Reality-striving is hard.
Getting it right is not a childish task.
There are places the brain
Wants to go – light and easy, where butterflies and blue
Abound– but what is reality? Or is it,
What are realities?

6.23

For example, the fathomless enigma of Time.
Time is not a stream but seems to be. Consider how
The roll of Earth makes it seem to us the sun moves up
At dawn. Such illusions are understandable and common.
And, we must note, when we don't know it's an illusion,
We think we know but it's not so. We are biology
Happening, changing, while watching change –
Everything changing. We call this Time. Its lexicon
Is illusion-laced.

6.24

We never experience the future because it's always not yet
Happening. It's expectation that change will occur,
A brain function embedded into the forming of us,
Aware of possibilities of more will come,
Or no more. We don't even know when the present is,
Because it's merely a door through which the future
Changes presto-fast from a will-be prospect
Into a what-was memory. The door is too thin,
And it has no way to close.

6.25

The past is what? It does not exist. Past tense is past tense.
It's only memory as Life's museum built by the present,
Connecting the non-existing future to the non-existing past,
Which goes through the door of the mirage present,
An ever-open door through which future, like a rabbit,
Goes by the wink of a magician's wand in just a blink.
Does the present even blink?

6.26

We go from here to there when all that's happened is we go
From here to there. Time did not pass. No Time stream flows.
The spot I see is not what was – it's new. We stare
At the same spot and it seems the same, just as we feel
That from moment to moment we are the same.
Coping with the fundamentals of just being alive
Requires that we ignore what's really happening,
So we can survive.

6.27
Time, how elusively all things change, making it seem
That something mystical is passing, which we call Time.
Not like water from the palm; not like silk threads slipping
Through a tangle; not like the breeze fluttering the leaves.
No, as silent as stars glittering at night, and fading
At dawn. Into that ocean of past, where all is going,
The same never-ending slow pouring out. It can be felt,
Somehow, from inside – the passing, the silence,
Always going,
Forever gone.

6.28
Our brains and views developed to see an environment
Of scale and pace with which our activities, like lock and key,
Can form functioning ways. We know when a tree is falling,
But do not know when a microbe inside our body is dying.
A star is a firefly in the night. The Earth is flat from here
To there, the land on which we stand. How could we know
It's a sphere, larger by far than we could imagine.

6.29
But Man, with dreams as brave as David's sling,
By imagination, myths, thinking, reasoning, effort,
Came upon eureka, called the Scientific Method,
Such that he has become the modern Modern Man
Who crosses mountains, sails across oceans, flies
Through skies, rockets to the moon and beyond,
Invents technology like a cornucopia.
Lucy, what do you think of that?

6.30

Here we are. We are born, without a request
Or intention. We live, trying to understand our environment,
Time, emotions, survival, Life itself. Then there's death
To deal with. All is chunked into us like rag dolls
Rolling down an assembly line. Overarching this morass
Of our Life experiences is the question: What's going on?
What is this whole process? Can we know?

6.31

No one, utterly, absolutely no one
Can deal with death, when the end ends,
As though it's nothing. Existence itself is impossible
To imagine, but then, once existence is a fact, the end
Of it cannot be. The brain, a program once in motion,
Wants to continue its mode, projecting a future, life life life,
Beyond what is clearly the end. Existence is not programmed
To contemplate non-existence.

6.32

Fear death? But don't count out denial. Our minds
Are hugely complicated, layers of reality woven
Into layers of denial, so the system can operate.
Minute by minute, day by day, we go our way
Knowing we will die, but that's too hard to know.
Whistling in the dark so we can go on.

6.33

A life becomes connected with other lives, often
With extraordinary closeness, like parent-child,
Spouse, sibling, friend – and yet this connection
Is broken, terminated, severed, by death. That dear person
Is gone, never again to re-appear. This is the death
With which we must come to terms, to try,
The best we can.

6.34

But any parting can be final. How many people
Were encrusted inside of us, and then a parting came,
With forever as its name? Even the faces in a crowd,
Along the streets – we can see one time only. Sometimes
There is a fleeting pause, eyes connect, or a few words said,
Then, like the press of a button,
Gone.

6.35

See that photo of a large group. One face there
Is dearly known. But it is a photo, nothing more.
And it merely opens a memory cell of material-matter brain,
Where skin and smile and emotions have slumbered.
This photo of this face, this memory inside this brain,
This past gone through this present door where we think
A moment of future lingers, walking through us,
Without a nod.

6.36

Think deep, how Man is what he is. And nothing more.
Sure that's a lot, but also it's not much,
Compared, let's say, to all of Life,
Or all of the Universe, or even smaller bits –
A galaxy, a rose garden, a flock of geese,
A single anything that is –
Is that a lot, or not?

6.37

All the men women children running about –
Teeming, laughing, solemn and sad, gay and glad.
We never asked to be here – not one, not any.
We emerge from that muck mixing with luck,
Like one fine day we awake and look about
And say out loud we're here.
Now what do we do?

6.38

Myths, fables, fairy tales, good science, bad science, a lot
To choose from. It might have been that we don't care, like,
Maybe, the worm, the bacterium. But we do. What's going on,
We ask. Why do we bother to ask? How do you explain
The mechanism by which Evolution hit upon a thing?
If it works it gets play, and the kick that Man receives
From his curiosity has been a driver of immense power.
The thirst for sweet knowledge –
What a thirst!

6.39

We are peas in pods, all alike but never any two alike -
Prairie critters, mountain creatures, aviators, sailors,
Explorers, scientists, builders, musicians, poets, painters,
Sculptors, raconteurs. We write, we sing, we dance,
We're sick and well and happy and sad. Who are we
Who ask and plead? Who are we who hope and never stop?
Who are we who have so little that we can do,
Who can only do what we can do?

6.40

Evolution, you are a con artist. You make us think
That we do it, although we have nothing to do with it!
You conjured us from smoke and mirrors, a skin-wrapped
Bundle, and put in everything that's in it,
Including the delusion
We had something to do with what it is. When will I realize
That when I get hungry,
It's not because I choose it?

6.41

We can do what we wish, they say. Just anything.
But look around and catalogue. Eat, sleep, procreate,
Work, some play, some thrills, some frills. But realize
The list is finished soon. Just do anything you wish?
But your wishing is on this list. Try wishing
For wishes that are not inside the human bounds.

6.42

Mosquito, what's your catalogue? Or fruit fly?
Or turtle? We know you well, your origin, your habitat,
Your behavior, your procreation. We can even see your future,
The battle you fight. You are what's written, and must stay
Within your cage. You're fixed and pinned to be your thing,
And that alone. And humans? We can rise to see
What we are. We too are fixed and caged
Within the bounds of humanness.

6.43

My cat sleeps a lot, curled contentedly, noticing only
When he feels like it. I ask, what are your needs?
He gets fed. He's too old to care to play. Nature's way
Is to find the path with the least expenditure of energy.
Kangaroos hop for that reason. Man can run
Longer and farther than apes.
Life's that way. Find food, eat, copulate. Man
Has a few other frills. But Life's that way. Just the agenda
That keeps survival in the focus.

6.44

What did Evolution do to us? Installed every part. Wrote
My agenda? Handed to me my list of wishes and dreams?
Put this pen in my hand? Where is anything that I do? I heard
That we have built robots, pre-programed everything,
In the finest details, and set them loose. We hid beneath
The circuit boards the part that deludes them to believe
They themselves originate.

6.45

Well, it's certainly true that most of what we think and do
Was founded, built and honed by the Evolution factory,
All of the really basic things, like hunger, thirst, sex,
Aggression, fight or flight, sleep, dreams, moods – the list
Of just the basics is too long. I must put consciousness
On the list – it's sine qua non. And mental and emotional
Variations. Oh Lord, it is true, isn't it?
Everything that counts?

6.46

Free will or determinism? I go to the philosophers and ask.
It's so easy to see that everyone does what he does
Because that's what he would do. He's been bundled
And programed, like a bee. Can you say what that lion
Will do, hungry and sniffing the smell of game?
What's calling to him, to have him listen, and decide?

6.47

What is free will? The rules of the game of being human
Embrace us closely to hold us on the required course.
Within the rules, we can play with intent and chance.
We can fidget within the unremitting rules, wiggle
Our desires and efforts, and those decisions are decisions
That we make, or so we think. How much does it matter?
If we think we have free will, we have free will.

6.48

Free will? Yes and no. Not to control the galaxies, stars,
Our sun. Or the moon, though we can touch it.
The Earth itself, yes, which we're riding hard.
I think of a football game, in which we have choices
And variations on minute-by-minute behavior.
This is free will. But it's football we're playing,
And that's not for us to decide.

6.49

Rules, some hard, some soft, some transient, some known.
We have free will to play this game we're born into.
If free will means power to affect some matters
But not everything, with success or not, or small,
Or great, beset by variables, then, within that knotted context,
You and I, sitting and talking one evening, we may say
Is my life course pre-determined? *Am I the master of my fate?*
Am I the captain of my soul?

6.50

The prisoner will rise and face the bench. You are accused
Of having nothing beyond your bound-in humanness.
How do you plead? Guilty or not guilty? Not guilty?
Then speak.
Your honor, I present as evidence the simple case
Of music. Before modern humans, what was it
And its boundaries? When we arrived, your honor, look
At what we wrought. Has our creativity flooded
Beyond our boundaries?

6.51

The reason why we humans create such wonderful art
Is simply the wonder and not knowing. Each little one
Of us receives piercing streams and stings telling us
This is the world. It's ours while we live. Each of us somehow
Came into it alive, and it will continue after each of us is gone.
Each of us, a being, a flame from the void, to come and go.

6.52

This presents great puzzlement, confusion, met with effort
To figure it out. What's left is to sober up on fantastic
Experiences we are having from the liquor of art. Let it ask,
Seek, depict, reflect, shine, astound, instruct, weep, keen,
Laugh, cry, love, hate, contemplate – it's us about us.
These iterations keep on depicting us and our condition,
Helping us to face and sort this thing.
We are here, this place and time. We must say something.
This is our way of being what we are.

6.53

The above, written yesterday, thinking about it, perhaps
Dreaming about it – it's far too capsulized, even hubristic.
Art is rich and varied, more than can be said, but the point
Is, its theme is the same. No matter the genre, the theme
Is its driver, its message, its anguish. It's one theme,
Man's yearn to know about himself, the subject of this poem.
Where did we come from? Who are we? What is this?
Yes, beauty and shock are in it, but we are all weaving
The same cloth.

6.54

And so it is with Mankind itself. Take ten human beings
At random from all around the globe, or a hundred
Or a thousand. All the same. Let them look at each other,
Squarely in the eye, with truth and honesty burning like
A branding iron. Have each one write down, briefly, who he is,
His view of Life, his agenda. What is written will be the same.
Different languages, of course. Different clothes, of course.
But

6.55

If – here's the logic – if from inside we cannot see inside
Then how are humans supposed to see who humans are?
We conjure up aliens in shapes and sizes – but see how human
They are? We are biologically like so many animals,
But so far apart. If we would know what humans are
We must step outside. Gödel showed you cannot prove
A system from within the system.

6.56

Even when we make aliens in our fantasies,
Even ones arriving here, we say, you're strange.
But look at them. The limit of all we can imagine
Describes them close like us, ourselves. Are there more
Aliens in Rain Forests than in our imagination?
Our imagination is also bound inside our cage.

6.57

As we look at us, we can isolate to an individual life,
Its own tight bundle, many are the songs, poems, paintings,
Stories that do just that. The heartache, the success,
The loneliness, the strands of hair, the color of the eyes,
The baby's first cry, the gurgle and gasp at her last breath,
The parting, the embrace – tell me, how much can
One life contain? This is the thrall of our quotidian fascination
With ourselves.

6.58

Or let's just glance at the sociology of group behavior.
Some groups claim superiority, showing others it's true,
Through race, gender, caste, slavery, war, genocide –
All the ills of power and abuse,
Warps of cultural attitudes, wealth
And employment, disparities, weird and fate-misfortunes
Of illnesses, deformities, roulette mental capabilities, how
We deal with these, and these among us. The ideal
Is not even ever really serious in our minds. Even
How it could be done is darkness.

6.59

What's it like to be Man-alive? There are no comparisons.
What we are was delivered as a pre-fabricated package.
Nor all thy Piety nor Wit shall cancel half a Line,
Nor all thy Tears wash out a Word of it. This is our blessing
And our burden. The bad, the good, the ugly, the beautiful.
Except, Man is changing the rules of Evolution. Coming to us
Is a future far different from what brought us here.

WHERE ARE WE GOING?

Into this Universe, and Why not knowing,
Nor Whence, like Water willy-nilly flowing:
And out of it, as Wind along the Waste,
I know not Whither, willy-nilly blowing.

Rubaiyat of Omar Khayyam, V*erse 29*
(Fourth Edition, Fitzgerald translation)

7.1

There you are, a baby, a child, a teenager. You see
The world, family, personal relations, school, seasons,
Growth, death, your own struggle to know.
They tell you a lot but how do you discern?
What do you do, what do humans do, who are we?

7.2

Well, the sun is a nuclear furnace, galaxies are points
Of light. Life on Earth is new, and Man is still crossing
The threshold. Matter and energy are the same
At the bottom, but they unfold a reality that is weird,
Beautiful, orderly, comprehensible mostly it seems.
Now, your job is to go figure it out, and to figure out
Along the way, how did you get here.
Whence? What? Whither?

7.3

Physics can describe the world, everything
In it, its origin and destination, all we need to know,
Except: what's going on. Newton's physics gave it
A big push. Also, pitching in – astronomy, biology,
Medical science, chemistry, geology, technology.
A mad rush toward knowledge, more and more.
Man flying.

7.4

Your future? You think a lot about it, preparing
For it, as it becomes your past, like rushing water.
One life, short, or long, depending on how you want
To frame it. Against what background and foreground?
You are always your past, present and future.
Your weather. Your motion along the timeline.
Change is its name.

7.5

Do you think that's a job, thinking what your future holds?
The years from your birth, the time remaining, probabilities
And possibilities and some things you never could have
Thought? Haunted by the mystery of being, the raveling
And unraveling. On the grassy bank, you look
Into the reflecting pool of water,
And then to the sky, and you ask,
What, when, where, why, am I?

7.6

Well, think of Mankind, the whole of it, and wonder
Where are we going? Evolution progressing to now,
Out of a swampy, microbial murk, to what we see now.
Wonders of Mankind on a binge of knowledge-seeking,
Population exploding, materialism, consumption,
Overrunning the planet, our only home, our lifeline.
There are voices of wisdom drowning in wars, poverty.
And global warming that points us straight and maybe soon
To becoming a Venus.

7.7

Evolution. Is this your handiwork? Thou giveth
And taketh away. Are we helpless players in a play
Being written as we perform it? Is there no script?
Can we have a revolt of the players? Yes, we are doing it
Now! Evolution, you made a mistake. You developed us
And gave us the power to see how it works,
To take charge of ourselves, to take away the reins
From you, a witless maker of miracles, to take hold
Of the reins, to hold them in our own hands.

7.8

Is this true? Man is beginning to decide for himself
What Evolution will do, the child becoming adult,
Saying, move aside, we will now take charge?
Oh, do be careful what you wish for. What if
It comes to be real? It will be the greatest event
Since Creation! It's already happening.

7.9

Let's engage in a fantasy, or nightmare.
Reaching perfection of what we can do,
Manipulating genes, clipping, fusing,
Adding, subtracting, eliminating all the negatives –
No more disease, no pouting or writer's block - -
All that's left is skill, creativity, solutions,
Beauty, brilliance - - -

7.10

Until, at last, using cloning as a multiplier,
Replicating on and on, we have it perfect.
We become perfect, all alike, every gene
And every atom of every gene, replicating
Without flaw, all alike, perfectly all alike.
All of our experiences will be alike,
Orwellian over the top, all alike.

7.11

The theater of the absurd, but it helps
To see the point, that our future may veer
Like a rocket in the night sky to be absurd,
A place not now inside our crystal ball.
Even so, that would not be an end of the future,
For the future would go on and on. They
Would wonder deeply about their future,
All of them.

7.12

But we are doing it. Understanding genes,
All the pieces, the plots and flaws, the wheels
That run the machine, and how to intervene.
Now, ponder the agenda. What would you like?
Rid us of all diseases? Rid us of dying?
All are beautiful. All are intelligent. All
Have become what we wish we could become.

7.13

Not in a year, of course, nor the lifetimes
Of those of us who are guilty of doing this.
What do you think about a hundred years?
What will be our power to manipulate who we are
A thousand years from now? Does anyone
Have enough vision to see such a vision?
It's unlikely our future will be nothing but more
Of the same, forever. The future of our past
Was never that way.

7.14

And all the conundrums that come with it!
Change a brain into one that thinks about
Changing the brain, so that the new brain
. . .Can do. . .what? Man made by Man
Just like Man would want Man to be.
Got it, sir. But tell me,
What is that?

7.15

Part re-modeled Man is where we start,
Which we're doing now. Transplants of hearts,
Kidneys. Soon – we see this happening – anything
Can be made to repair, replace anything.
Prostheses like hips, knees, legs, arms, lens.
Soon it's anything. Every person you meet:
How much of you is the original you?
Will we, someday,
Start from scratch?

7.16

And with life eternal, or even simply very long,
Where shall we put all these human beings?
Even worse, do we stop making new ones?
No more babies? Or, if so, only by yet-unknown rules
Of supply and demand. Take a look at infants and children
And tell me, honestly, would you change the system
To a perfect one that produces
No more infants and children?

7.17

Can you imagine? Deciding how many people
Is the right number? How could our decision-making
Process ever perform that feat? Today we can't decide
A number or manage the process if we could decide.
How much stress will this old Earth endure? What kind
Of Earth will our future Earth be?
It will not be what we have today.

7.18

This Earth in all its human-recorded history
Is having now an identity crisis – slow
By the Man Calendar but by Universe Time,
I'll bet its pace is fast. It's our space ship
That we're riding, most likely
The only one we can ever have.

7.19

But, you quickly say, all of our wishes were installed
By the old-school Evolution. Will this coming superman
Change even that? What we wish for, what gives
Us pleasure, in short, what we want and don't want, do
And not do. Will we set our new agenda? I hear music,
I see scenes, I read language, I hold babies.
I know what I want.

7.20

But, oh, there is a rub. Turns out, a big one. Man arose
Enormously higher than all his kindreds that still ply
Their struggles with tooth and claw. But Man brought
With him the tools and schemes developed to negotiate
The savannah and forest animal ways. His DNA,
Reptilian brain, fight or flight, all his lusts and
Slaughtering skills – as though

7.21

Transported into another world where the useful
Golden rules are new for us, but we bring baggage
We could not leave behind. We've gotten a lot of new bags
For our fresh new journeys, but they're hard-tied
To the old as well. We've blended, our new and old.
Shining on us is new light
While our past is casting shadows,
Making us both a this and a that.

7.22

We are a perishable thing, but not yet perished.
Making high gains already to understand
Some of the biological structures and workings
Of the jigsaw puzzles of ourselves that meandered
And twisted amazing pathways used by us to cope
And improve, building mechanisms and instincts
That got us this far. The stuff ingrained in our beginnings,
Is what we must rend, blend, re-direct, to excise out

7.23

Some of those wondrous savage nursery skills
That prod us still to kill each other, and our beautiful
Fellow beasts. And to learn our Earth can be killed
By our own hands. To ward off disasters large and small,
For the few billion years remaining. The Earth has not always
Been inhabitable by the likes of us. How powerful
And disciplined can we possibly become? Falling short
Would be – well – falling short.

7.24

New horizons beckon us with bountiful visions.
New horizons seen from a luscious Earth.
New Horizons nestling us with Evolution's grand gifts
To bask in the wonderment and joy of flowers, trees,
Blossoms and bees, cool rains, mountain streams,
Sunrises, sunsets, skies of blue, dark nights
Deep with stars, and a moon that at times
Can take you to your knees.

7.25

If I were an ant, or bee, or dog, or horse, I would know
What I want. I would want to be me. So it is, I think,
With us humans. All we want is to smooth the edges
Of what we are, and to have it longer and longer.
We're only looking for fixes to the thing we are,
And we are not dreaming to become something else.

7.26

But the thought occurs – we only eliminate what we know
We don't want. So, no wars, no crime, no disease,
No fears, no loneliness, no craving and yearning. Whoa!
Wait just a minute! Isn't that what creates the music,
The art, the literature, the inventions? Is pain not a worker
Of miracles? Is suffering not what makes our dreams?
You would make
A man who has no dreams?

7.27

Enough already. Back to the more manageable topic:
Where are we going? Let's parse that a little? Short run?
Or long run? I submit we know more about the long run
Than the short run. We can talk about escaping the Earth
Before the flood, or being consigned to oblivion. We know
That day will come. Cosmology lays it out
Clear and simple.

7.28

First, the short run. Since we have no crystal ball, cannot
Read tea leaves, or the entrails of birds, we don't know much.
And the more we don't know, the less useful
The talk. We will have war and rumors of war, famine,
The poor will be with us always, wonders of computers,
Science, books without end – how long is the list of more
Of the same? Over time, the same is not the same,
But seems so, because the stream of Time flows like
Slow motion.

7.29

I want to say to you, I have invented a box. You get inside,
Set the dial to the number of years from now, the time
You choose now to wake up in the future, alive and well,
To see what has happened in the interim to Life on Earth.
It's safe, without any doubt that it will function perfectly.
Now this will really test your vow of curiosity.

7.30

Say goodbye to all your family, your friends, the life
You know. It's a trade-off. You can choose to stick
To your life, and die, or get in the box, set the dial.
Whoops! To what future time? A mere hundred years,
Or, be brave, a thousand years? Or crazy-brave,
A million years? The box will drift with continents,
Get lobbed about by civilizations that come and go.
It may encounter extreme heat or cold. When it opens,
It may open to desolation. The short-run time
Of a million years may be beyond our time on Earth.

7.31

That's our problem when thinking about the future of man
In the short-run. How short or long is the short-run?
We can perform like high-wire equilibrists when denial
Is the act. Ask Noah about that problem. Will we have
Our Noah? Calamities, catastrophes, plagues, wildly
Spreading diseases, they will come, and, as usual,
We'll go on. Or, it really could happen, an asteroid,
Or passing beyond global warming's point of no return.

7.32

Well, there's your short-run, more of the same
That's not the same but is the same, or the short-run
Becomes the long-run because the end comes
Faster than what cosmology has in its mind
To deliver to us in its version of the long-run.

7.33

When it's over? Could be like many things
That end. Listening to a music siege, reading
A book – not wanting it to end. But it does.
A relationship can come to an end, and does,
Because of death or something else. My own death,
My very own. I will not know the experience, because
I am the end that ends.

7.34

Well, this world will end. Stars end. Planets end.
Life on planets ends, at least at the planet's end.
Life on Earth of course will end. Who among you
Wants to raise a denial hand? Oh, how sweet
Denial is. Thus, we can continue on our merry way.
Don't think about it. Even if true. Coping is a must.
Gather ye rosebuds while ye may.

7.35

This planet Earth is a living organism held in place
By many many symbiotic pieces, interacting,
Linked, dependent upon each other, the process
By which the Earth breathes, stays alive. What if
Something vital goes astray, veers away, like
Global warming or some other critical part.

7.36

A fish inside a tank is inside its total world,
And Man lives inside his tank. Much bigger,
But a closed system. Maintaining the equilibrium
Of a fish tank requires knowledge, care and attention.
The Earth is also precariously balanced. We've always
Regarded Earth as a stable background,
Forever sustaining Life.
Surely we are learning that this is not so.

7.37

The end of Planet Earth? In five billion years
For sure, but the end of Life may be sooner.
Maybe there will be enough time to build an ark
To go to another planet – and we are learning about many.
The travel time? The fastest spacecraft known
Today would need hundreds of generations
To reach the star nearest to Earth – whose planets,
If any, probably would not sustain
The likes of us.

7.38

When sons and daughters boarded the Mayflower
With other Pilgrims, the trip was several weeks
To a destination of *terra firma*. Sure, the Pilgrims could
Not look back, and the tears of friends and family
At dockside
Were real and final.

7.39

Intra-solar exploration is one thing but
Interstellar travel is far too long. What's
The point of boarding a spacecraft with a genetic pool
Of human beings so the descendants so far removed
Can land somewhere, if all goes well? Somewhere
Among the distant stars – would this be a rescue
Of humankind and our Earth-made civilization?

7.40

Maybe so, in a way. Just point to an identified
Earth-like planet, use space ships with futuristic speed,
Plans for many launches. Some of us may make it,
Taking with us some of who we are. There are things
Out there in our far distant future, so far over
The horizon of time and chance,
Our legs and minds go wobbly.

7.41

How much of our humanity is portable? Really,
Does it matter? Just basic stuff with which to start
The engines. Pilgrims packed their ships with seeds,
Fowl, animals, tools and books. Their hands
Were packed with skills, their minds with knowledge
And dreams, their hearts with yearning and love.

7.42

When we launch our ships someday – if that's our way,
And if we're able – to send our seeds to another planet,
Much and many will be left behind for the cataclysm.
For a while our fondest hopes and wishes
Will be in their sails, and then good night.
There will be nothing of us remaining
To tell our tale, full of our sound and fury
Signifying everything.

END

THANKS

I say a special thanks to Nick Courtright, poet, teacher, editor, gifted poet, for working me and this project to its conclusion. As often acknowledged, and indeed true in this case, I could not have done it without him.

Also I feel a need to express a universal gratitude to the legions of scientists, writers, teachers, governments, philanthropists – on and on – who pursued and brought forth – and are still doing so – the cornucopia of exploration and knowledge about who we are, our place in the universe, and all that is mankind's achievement. All of it, a boundless gift to countless people like me.

THE AUTHOR

William Guest graduated from Yale University in 1953, and Harvard Law School in 1957. A practicing attorney from 1957 - 1985, he was chair and CEO of a life insurance enterprise engaged in acquisitions from 1985 - 2006. Poetry and sculpting is his third career.

His poems have appeared in venues such as *The New Lantern Review, Calliope, Storyteller Magazine,* and *Weight of Addition: An Anthology of Texas Poetry.* He is also a juried poet in *The Houston Poetry Fest.*

Guest is a South Carolina native and long-time resident of Houston, Texas. He is a life member of the Philosophical Society of Texas, the Houston Philosophical Society, and the Board of Visitors of McDonald Observatory, as well as a member of the Houston Board of Nature Conservancy, and an Advisory Director of Public Poetry.

Beyond *Who Are We*, Guest is also the author of a book of travel journals (Antarctica, the Arctic, Peru and the Amazon Basin, and the Yeats Poetry Festival in Sligo, Ireland) to be published by Lamar University Press.